Nimitz Class Aircraft C...

On Deck®

Written by Jim Goodall

Cover Art by Don Greer

Line Illustrations by Matheu Spraggins

Squadron/Signal

About the Walk Around®/On Deck Series®

The Walk Around®/On Deck® series is about the details of specific military equipment using color and black-and-white archival photographs and photographs of in-service, preserved, and restored equipment. *Walk Around®* titles are devoted to aircraft and military vehicles, while *On Deck®* titles are devoted to warships. They are picture books of 80 pages, focusing on operational equipment, not one-off or experimental subjects.

Copyright 2009 Squadron/Signal Publications
1115 Crowley Drive, Carrollton, TX 75006-1312 U.S.A.
Printed in the U.S.A.

ISBN 978-0-89747-605-8

(Front Cover) The USS NIMITZ (CVN 68) first deployed on 7 July 1976, departing Norfolk in a task force with the nuclear-powered cruisers USS SOUTH CAROLINA (CGN 37) and USS CALIFORNIA (CGN 36) for a seven-month tour of duty. For the first time in 10 years nuclear-powered ships deployed to the Mediterranean. In November 1976, the Commander, Naval Air Forces Atlantic Fleet gave NIMITZ the Battle "E" as the most efficient carrier in the Atlantic Fleet. NIMITZ returned to Norfolk on 7 February 1977.

(Back Cover) USS GEORGE WASHINGTON (CVN 73), the sixth ship in the NIMITZ - class of carriers and the fourth Navy ship to bear the name, leaves Norfolk on 7 April 2008 *en route* to Yokosuka, Japan, becoming the first nuclear-powered aircraft carrier to be forward deployed.

Military/Combat Photographs and Snapshots

If you have any photos of aircraft, armor, soldiers, or ships of any nation, particularly wartime snapshots, please share them with us and help make Squadron/Signal's books all the more interesting and complete in the future. Any photograph sent to us will be copied and returned. Electronic images are preferred. The donor will be fully credited for any photos used. Please send them to:

Squadron/Signal Publications
1115 Crowley Drive
Carrollton, TX 75006-1312 U.S.A.
www.SquadronSignalPublications.com

(Title Page) The aircraft carrier USS *Abraham Lincoln* (CVN 72) transits the Indian Ocean with the Arleigh Burke-class guided-missile destroyer USS Russell (DDG 59) and the Oliver Hazard Perry-class guided-missile frigate USS Curts (FFG 38) on 5 September 2008. The Abraham Lincoln Strike Group is on a scheduled deployment in the U.S. 7th Fleet area of responsibility operating in the western Pacific and Indian oceans. (Mass Communication Specialist 2nd Class James R. Evans / U.S. Navy)

Dedication

To the youth of America, the 18 to 24 year olds who truly do keep the mighty Nimitz Class CVNs operating, my heartfelt thanks go to our military and to the greatest Nation on earth, the United States of America.............Thank you for your service.

Introduction

The Nimitz Class CVN aircraft carrier continues to be the centerpiece of the forces necessary for forward presence. Whenever there has been a crisis, the first question has been: "Where are the carriers?" Carriers support and operate aircraft that engage in attacks in the air, on the sea, and on the shore targeting those who threaten free use of the sea. They also engage in sustained operations in support of other forces.

The Nimitz Class CVN aircraft carriers are deployed worldwide in support of U.S. interests and commitments. They can respond to global crises in ways ranging from peacetime presence to full-scale war. Together with their on-board air wings, the carriers have vital roles across the full spectrum of conflict.

The 10 operational Nimitz-class carriers, including the just-commissioned USS *George H. W. Bush* (CVN 77), are the largest warships in the world. USS Nimitz (CVN 68) was the first to undergo its initial refueling during a 33-month Refueling Complex Overhaul at Northrup Grumman Shipbuilding in 1998. The next generation of carrier, the GERALD R. FORD Class (the lead ship hull number will be CVN 78), started construction in 2007 and is slated to be delivered in 2015 to replace USS Enterprise (CVN 65). Construction of the CVN 79 (not yet named) is programmed to begin in 2012 and to be placed in commission in 2018.

The 41st President of the United States, George H.W. Bush, and the prospective commanding officer of the *George H. W. Bush* aircraft carrier (CVN 77), Captain Kenin E. O'Flaherty, both placed a personal set of naval aviator wings under the 700-ton island superstructure of the vessel on 8 July 2006. The aviator wings were used to symbolize a naval custom called "stepping the mast," which dates from antiquity and consists of placing coins under the step or bottom of a ship's mast during construction.

Acknowledgments

Capt. Patrick D. Hall, Captain, (CO) USS Abraham Lincoln (CVN 72)

Capt. Thomas E. Nosenzo, Executive Office (OX) USS Abraham Lincoln (CVN 72)

LCDR Kathy Sandoz, PAO for the USS Abraham Lincoln (CVN 72)

LT Rick "Top Cat" Escalante, V-2 Division Officer USS Abraham Lincoln (CVN 72)

MC3 Jim Evans Ships, Photographer USS Abraham Lincoln (CVN 72)

MC3 Nick Morton, Photographer USS Abraham Lincoln (CVN 72)

LT Matthew Galan, COMPACFLT, Public Affairs

LCDR Elizabeth A Meydenbauer Commander, Naval Air Forces Assistant PAO (CNAF)

Mike Dillard, Photo Library Editor, Northrop Grumman Shipbuilding

To all of the Navy's exceptional photographers, way too many to list. Wherever possible, I have given all photographers proper photo credit.

http://www.navsource.org/archives: One of the best ship reference sites on the net.

The 700-ton bow unit, the final keel section of the Nimitz-class aircraft carrier *George H. W. Bush* (CVN-77) is lowered into place in the dry dock at Northrop Grumman Newport News shipyard on 8 March 2005. *George H. W. Bush* was built using modular construction: small sections of the ship below the waterline are lowered into place in dry dock. CVN-77 was the second carrier to have the new bulbous bow design that adds buoyancy to the forward end of the ship and improves hull efficiency

The USS *George H. W. Bush* (CVN 77) superstructure waits its turn to be hoisted into position on the flight deck for final assembly in November 2005. (John Whalen / Northrop Grumman)

The massive twin rudders of the Nimitz class carrier, the USS *George H. W. Bush,* are positioned on the floor of Dry Dock 12 at the Northrop Grumman Newport News Shipbuilding's vast facilities in Newport News, Virginia, in June 2004. (Chris Oxley / Northrop Grumman)

Lights illuminate the job site for night-shift workers as construction of the USS *George H. W. Bush* (CVN 77) goes on around the clock in December 2005. Much of the work done at night is nearly the same kind of work that takes place during the day, but the night also affords the yard the chance to take care of some jobs that are difficult to do when more people around. X-ray-type testing of welds on piping and aircraft launching systems must be done at night. (Chris Oxley/ Northrop Grumman)

The bow of the USS *George H. W. Bush* (CVN 77), the last of the 10 Nimitz class carriers, sits in the dry dock at the Northrop Grumman Newport News Shipbuilding, Newport News, Virginia, in November 2005. (John Whalen / Northrop Grumman)

Aboard Pre Commissioning Unit USS *George H. W. Bush* (CVN 77), the last of 162 super lifts scheduled during the construction of the ship, places the 700-ton superstructure on the ship's flight Deck on 8 July 2006. CVN-77 the tenth and last Nimitz-class aircraft carrier was delivered to the U.S. Navy in early 2009. (U.S. Navy / Robert J. Stratchko)

The upper bow of Pre-Commissioning Unit *George H. W. Bush* (CVN 77) is lifted into place at Northrop Grumman Newport News shipyard in Virginia on 15 March 2006. CVN 77 is the 10th and last Nimitz-class aircraft carrier to be built. (John Whalen / Northrop Grumman)

Northrop Grumman Newport News Shipyard employees re-attach a propeller to the number-three shaft aboard the Nimitz-class aircraft carrier USS *George Washington* (CVN 73) on 23 July 2005. (U.S. Navy / Glen M. Dennis)

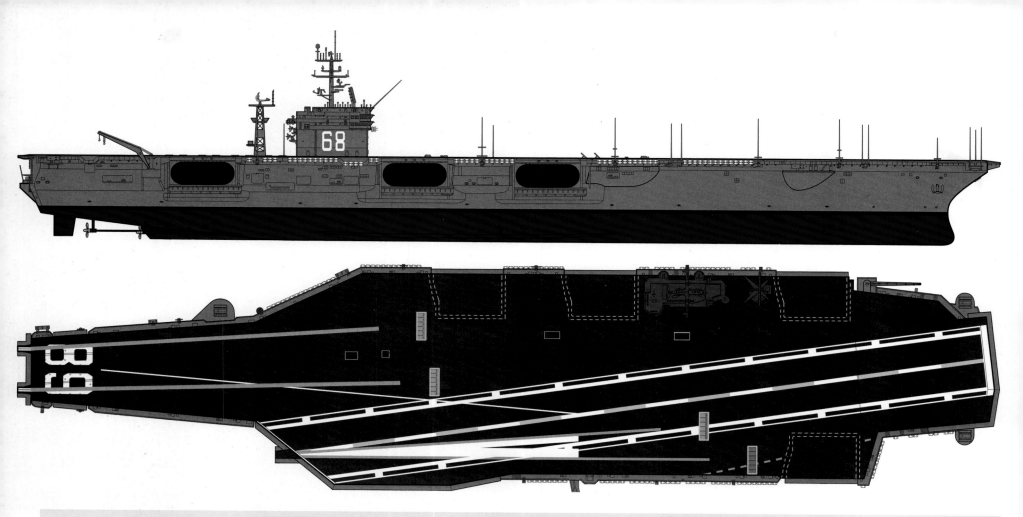

USS Nimitz Class (CVN 68) Specifications

Builder: Northrop Grumman Shipbuilding Company.
Power Plant: Two A4W reactors, four shafts
Length: 333m (1,092 ft.) overall
flight deck Width: 76.8m (252 ft)
Beam: 41m (134 ft)
Displacement: 97,000 tons (98,600 metric tons) full load
Speed: 30+ knots (56+ km/h)
Aircraft: 85 (current wings are closer to 64, including 48 tactical and 16 support aircraft)
Intended to operate aircraft currently including the F/A-18 Hornet, EA-6B Prowler, E-2 Hawkeye, C-2 Greyhound, SH/HH-60 Seahawk, and S-3 Viking for many missions including self defense, land attack and maritime strike.

Cost: about U.S. $4.5 billion each
Average Annual Operating Cost: U.S. $160 million
Service Life: 50 years
Crew: Ship's Company: 3,200 - Air Wing: 2,480
Armament:
NATO Sea Sparrow launchers: three or four (depends on modification)
20mm Phalanx CIWS mounts: Three on *Nimitz* and *Eisenhower* and four on *Vinson* and later ships of the class, except *Washington,* which has three.
RIM-116 Rolling Airframe Missile: Two on *Nimitz, Washington,* and *Reagan,* will be retrofitted to other ships as they return for RCOH.
Date Deployed: 3 May 1975 (*Nimitz*)

USS *Nimitz* (CVN 68) and USS *Ronald Reagan* (CVN 76) navigate alongside each other during routine training exercises off the southern California coast on 16 November 2004. (U.S. Navy / Elizabeth Thompson)

An SH-60F Sea Hawk helicopter assigned to Helicopter Antisubmarine Squadron (HS) 5 flies in the vicinity of the aircraft carrier USS *Dwight D. Eisenhower* (CVN 69) on 9 May 2009. The helicopter's tail is painted in the Navy digital camouflage design. *Eisenhower* and Carrier Air Wing Seven are deployed to the U.S. Naval Forces Central Command area of responsibility. (U.S. Navy / Cmdr. Jane Campbell)

The nuclear-powered aircraft carrier USS *Nimitz* (CVN 68) makes its way back to San Diego, California, after completing a two-week underway period on 24 March 2005. *Nimitz* and Carrier Strike Group 11 (CSG-11) were conducting a Joint Task Force Training Exercise (JTFEX) off the coast of Southern California. U.S. Navy / (Danielle M. Sosa)

The Nimitz-class aircraft carrier USS *Dwight D. Eisenhower* (CVN 69) transits the Atlantic Ocean on 17 April 2006. *Eisenhower* and embarked Carrier Air Wing Seven (CVW-7) were participating in Composite Training Unit Exercise (COMPTUEX). (U.S. Navy / Miguel Angel Contreras)

A utility boat assigned to the Nimitz-class aircraft carrier USS *Dwight D. Eisenhower* (CVN 69) pulls around her stern dock during small boat operations on 6 June 2005. It was the first time *Eisenhower* conducted underway-small-boat-operations since the ship completed her four-year, mid-life overhaul. (U.S. Navy / Paul Simonds)

The Nimitz-class aircraft carrier USS *Dwight D. Eisenhower* (CVN 69) conducts routine operations in the Atlantic Ocean on 28 July 2006. *Eisenhower* is underway participating in the Joint Task Force Exercise (JTFEX) Operations Bold Step, an exercise involving more than 16,000 service members from five countries. (U.S. Navy / Miguel Angel Contreras)

Nimitz-class aircraft carrier USS *Abraham Lincoln* (CVN 72) underway in the Western Pacific Ocean on 4 April 2008. *Lincoln* and embarked Carrier Air Wing (CVW) Two were underway on a scheduled seven-month deployment to the 5th Fleet area of responsibility. (U.S. Navy / James R. Evans)

The nuclear-powered aircraft carrier USS *Carl Vinson* (CVN 70) sails in the South China Sea completing seven months of a scheduled deployment on 16 August 2009. *Vinson* Carrier Strike Group is on an extended deployment in the Western Pacific. (U.S. Navy / Jonathan M. Cirino)

Two F/A-18C Hornets, assigned to the "Blue Diamonds" of Strike Fighter Squadron One Four Six (VFA-146), and two F/A-18F Super Hornets, assigned to the "Black Knights" of Strike Fighter Squadron One Five Four (VFA-154), perform a fly-by over USS *Carl Vinson* (CVN 70) to mark the completion of the final combat missions flown over Iraq for Carrier Air Wing Nine (CVW-9) on 30 June 2005. The *Carl Vinson* Carrier Strike Group was deployed to the Arabian Gulf conducting operations in support of multi-national forces in Iraq. The *Vinson* ended its deployment with a homeport shift to Norfolk, Virgina, and commenced a three-year refuel and complex overhaul. (U.S. Navy / Chris M. Valdez)

9

The nuclear powered aircraft carrier *Theodore Roosevelt* appears with her embarked Carrier Air Wing Eight (CVW-8) on 4 February 2003. *Roosevelt* is conducting training exercises in the Caribbean Sea while preparing to deploy to the United States Central Command Area of Responsibility. (U.S. Navy / Todd M. Flint)

F-14D Tomcats launch from the flight deck of Nimitz-class aircraft carrier USS *Theodore Roosevelt* (CVN 71) to their homeport of Naval Air Station Oceana on 10 March 2006. (U.S. Navy / Chris Thamann)

The nuclear-powered aircraft carrier USS *Dwight D. Eisenhower* (CVN 69) is seen underway alongside the battleship USS *New Jersey* (BB 62) on 29 September 1983. (U.S. Navy)

The Nimitz-class aircraft carrier USS *Theodore Roosevelt* (CVN 71) heads to sea following a logistics stop on the Greek island of Crete on 22 February 2006. *Roosevelt with* Carrier Air Wing Eight (CVW-8) were underway on a regularly scheduled deployment supporting maritime security operations. (U.S. Navy / Paul Farley)

An MH-60 "Knight Hawk" assigned to the "Providers" of Helicopter Combat Support Squadron Five (HC-5) assists with an underway replenishment (UNREP) with the Military Sealift Command (MSC) combat stores ship USNS *San Jose* (T-AFS 7) on 24 January 2002. (U.S. Navy / Kittie VandenBosch)

The Military Sealift Command (MSC) hospital ship USNS *Mercy* (T-AH 19) navigates alongside USS *Abraham Lincoln* (CVN 72) after arriving on station near Banda Aceh, Sumatra, Indonesia, on 3 February 2005. (U.S. Navy / Gabriel R. Piper)

USS *Abraham Lincoln* (CVN 72) approaches pier Alpha at Naval Station Everett after returning from nearly a 10-month deployment in support of Operations Enduring Freedom and Iraqi Freedom on 6 May 2003. (U.S. Navy / Scott Taylor)

USS *Abraham Lincoln* (CVN 72) prepares for flight operations in the Gulf of Alaska as part of the joint training exercise, "Northern Edge" 2002. Approximately 7,500 active-duty service personnel will train at military installations, ranges, and the port of Valdez during the multi-service exercise on 19 April 2002. (U.S. Navy / Kittie VandenBosch)

Air Department crew members remove the slot seal from catapult number one on the flight deck of the USS *George Washington* (CVN 73) on 13 May 2004. The rubber seal keeps foreign objects from entering and damaging the catapult when not in use. The Norfolk, Virginia-based aircraft carrier and embarked Carrier Air Wing Seven (CVW-7) deployed in support of Operation Iraqi Freedom (OIF). (U.S. Navy / Jessica Davis)

Safety Department's Leading Petty Officer watches turnover procedures with the Nimitz-class aircraft carrier USS *Carl Vinson* (CVN 70) from the fantail aboard the Nimitz-class aircraft carrier USS *Harry S. Truman* (CVN 75) on 19 March 2005. Prominent in the middle of the photo are two external fuel tanks for an EA-6B Prowler. The *Harry S. Truman* Carrier Strike Group had turned over its responsibilities in the Arabian Gulf to the USS *Carl Vinson* (CVN 70) Carrier Strike Group.(U.S. Navy)

Flight Deck Crew Jerseys

Blue Worn by Aircraft Handlers & Tractor Drivers (with Blue Helmet), Elevator Operators (with White Helmet), and by Aircraft Directors (with Yellow Helmet)

Brown Worn by Plane Captains (with Brown helmet) and by Helicopter Plane Captains (with Red Helmet)

Green Worn by Arresting/Catapult Crew (with Green Helmet), by Arresting/Catapult Officers (with Yellow Helmet), and by Replenishment Officers (with White Helmet)

An airman fuels an F/A-18 "Hornet" from Carrier Air Wing One Seven (CVW 17) on the ship's flight deck on 20 September 2002. The USS *George Washington* (CVN 73) was on a regularly scheduled deployment conducting combat missions in support of Operation Enduring Freedom. (U.S. Navy / Jason R. Zalasky)

Aviation Ordnancemen assigned to the ship's G3 division configure a 2,000 pound MK-84 bomb as Joint Direct Attack Munitions (JDAM), in one of the weapons magazines on 2 March 2002. The *Kennedy* and her embarked carrier air wing (CVW) are expected to relieve USS Theodore Roosevelt (CVN 71), and will conduct missions in support of Operation Enduring Freedom. (U.S. Navy / Jim Hampshire)

Many sailors participate in a joint effort to erect the flight deck barricade during an emergency landing barricade drill aboard USS *Abraham Lincoln* (CVN 72) on 3 January 2003. The barricade is used as a last resort for emergency recoveries of aircraft aboard ship. (U.S. Navy / Jennifer Nichols)

Red Worn by Ordnance/Crash Crew (with Red Helmets)

Purple Worn by Refuelers (with Purple Helmets)

White Worn by Safety/Medical/Transfer Crew (with White Helmets), by Landing Signals Officers (with No Helmet), and by Plane Inspectors (with Green Helmets)

Yellow Worn by Plane Directors/Landing Officers (with Yellow Helmets), and Catapult and Arresting Gear Crew (with Green Helmets)

USS *Nimitz* (CVN 68) and USS *Ronald Reagan* (CVN 76) navigate alongside each other during routine training exercises off the southern California coast on 16 November 2004. (U.S. Navy / Elizabeth Thompson)

The Nimitz-class aircraft carrier USS *Carl Vinson* (CVN 70) departs Naval Station Mariannas, Guam, after a four-day port visit on 25 February 2005. *Carl Vinson* is on a scheduled deployment and will arrive in Norfolk, Virginia, at its completion to prepare her for refueling and a complex overhaul. (U.S. Navy / Dusty Howell)

The Nimitz-class aircraft carrier USS *Harry S. Truman* (CVN 75) sails out of Souda harbor in Crete, Greece, following a four-day port visit to Greece's largest island on 8 November 2004. *Truman* and embarked Carrier Air Wing Three (CVW-3) were on a regularly scheduled deployment in support of the Global War on Terrorism. (U.S. Navy / Paul Farley)

USS *John C. Stennis* (CVN 74) steams off the coast of southern California on 17 March 2003. The ship is was conducting pilot carrier qualifications with T-45 "Goshawk" aircraft. T-45s are used for intermediate and advanced portions of the Navy/Marine Corps pilot training programs for jet carrier aviation and tactical strike mission instruction. Initial carrier qualifications are normally conducted on an Atlantic-based carrier within close range of the Navy's Meridian, Mississippi, and Corpus Christi, Texas, training facilities. The qualifications were moved to the Pacific, however, since Stennis is one of the few carriers not deployed to regions of conflict. (U.S. Navy / Joshua Word)

The Nimitz-class aircraft carrier USS *John C. Stennis* (CVN 74) transits through the Pacific Ocean on 14 March 2006. *Stennis* was conducting carrier qualifications off the coast of Southern California. (U.S. Navy / Paul J. Perkins)

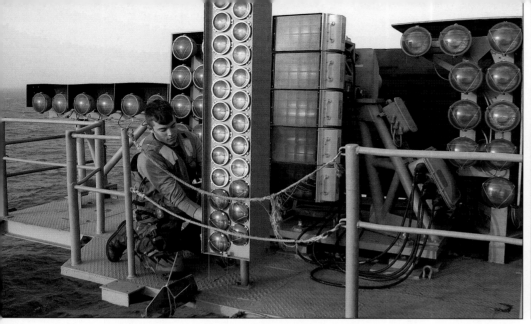

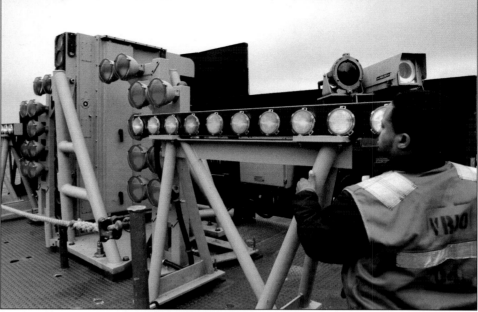

A U.S. Navy (USN) Interior Communications Electrician conducts maintenance on the Fresnel Lens Optical Landing System (FLOLS, the meatball) on 20 March 2003 FLOLS is a systems of lights that serve as a visual reference for pilots approaching to land aboard a carrier on station in the Arabian Gulf participating in Operation IRAQI FREEDOM. (U.S. Navy / Felix Garza, Jr)

An airman inspects the intensity of Datum Lights on the Improved Fresnel Lens Optical Landing System (IFLOLS) aboard the aircraft carrier USS *George Washington* (CVN 73) on 3 March 2001. Commanded by Captain Malcolm P. Branch, the *George Washington* was conducting sea trials in the western Atlantic following an unprecedented and highly successful six-month Planned Incremental Availability at Norfolk Naval Shipyard. (U.S. Navy / Kris White)

The Landing Signal Officers (LSO) of Attack Squadron Seventy-Five (VA-75) direct the approach of one of the squadrons A-6E aircraft during recovery (landing) operations on board the nuclear-powered aircraft carrier USS *George Washington* (CVN-73) on 26 March 1994. (U.S. Navy / Greg Snaza)

An overall view of the video display console and communications/data board of the Landing Signal Officers (LSO) work station on board the nuclear-powered aircraft carrier USS *George Washington* (CVN-73) on 26 March 1994. (U.S. Navy / Greg Snaza)

Supervisors watch attentively as a barricade is carefully lowered after a successful barricade drill aboard the USS *Abraham Lincoln* (CVN 72) on missions in the Western Pacific on 3 January 2003. Barricades are used as a last resort for emergency recoveries of aircraft aboard the ship. (U.S. Navy / Jennifer Nichols)

An aviation boatswain's mate places the launch bar of an F/A-18C Hornet of the "Knighthawks" of Strike Fighter Squadron One Three Six (VFA-136) into the shuttle of a catapult launch system aboard USS *George Washington* (CVN 73) on 2 May 2004. The Norfolk, Virginia-based carrier and embarked Carrier Air Wing Seven (CVW-7) were on a scheduled deployment backing Operation Iraqi Freedom. (U.S. Navy / Michael D. Blackwell II)

A sailor cleans the trough under a jet blast deflector on the flight deck of the USS *John C. Stennis* (CVN 74), on 18 May 2002. The John C. Stennis and its embarked Carrier Air Wing Nine (CVW-9) have been conducting combat missions in support of Operation Enduring Freedom and are en route to her homeport in San Diego, California. (U.S. Navy / Joshua Word)

A crash and recovery crane is parked on the flight deck of the nuclear-powered aircraft carrier USS *Abraham Lincoln* (CVN-72) on 19 January 1990. This crane replaces the NP-50 mobile cranes previously used aboard carriers of the Atlantic Fleet. (U.S. Navy / Tracy Lee Didas)

Crash-and-salvage personnel rig a training skeleton of an F-14 Tomcat to "Tilly" on 13 January 2005. "Tilly," a mobile crane used aboard all CVNs, is used to move damaged aircraft off the flight line during crash and salvage operations. The crash-and-salvage team serves as the ship's flight deck fire-fighting crew. (U.S. Navy / Bo Flannigan)

Sailors participate in a "Scrub Ex" on the flight deck aboard USS *George Washington* (CVN 73) on 18 December 2003, after the Air Wing assigned to Carrier Air Wing Seven (CVW-7) flew off, completing the Composite Training Unit Exercise (COMPTUEX) in the Atlantic Ocean. (U.S. Navy / Brien Aho)

Aviation ordnance men move an AGM-154 Joint Stand-Off Weapon (JSOW) from a weapons elevator onto the flight deck of the carrier USS *Nimitz* (CVN 68) on 27 March 2003. The Joint Standoff Weapon (JSOW) is a key program to replace five types of the older air-to-ground weapons in the naval inventory. The *Nimitz* and her embarked CVW-11 were operating with coalition forces in support of Operation Iraqi Freedom. (U.S. Navy / Bo Flannigan)

Aviation Ordinance men move an AIM-54C Phoenix long range air-to-air missile across the flight deck during preparations for flight operations aboard USS *George Washington* (CVN 73) on 19 November 1997. *George Washington* was in the Arabian Gulf to provide forward presence following Iraq's refusal to comply with UN weapons inspections. (U.S. Navy / Joseph Hendricks)

A bomb cart of Advanced Medium Range Air to Air Missiles (AMRAAM) sits in front of an F/A-18C "Hornet" assigned to the "Fist of the Fleet" of Strike Fighter Squadron Twenty-Five (VFA-25) aboard USS *Abraham Lincoln* (CVN 72), on 11 February 2003. VFA-25 is embarked with Carrier Air Wing Fourteen aboard *Lincoln* conducting operations in support of Operation Southern Watch. (U.S. Navy / Philip A. McDaniel)

U.S. Navy Aviation Ordnancemen (AO) move AIM-9 Sidewinder short range, IR (infrared) missiles from a weapons elevator on to the flight deck of the nuclear powered aircraft carrier USS *George Washington* (CVN 73) on 7 February 1998. The *George Washington* and Carrier Air Wing One (CVW-1) are conducting operations in the Arabian Gulf in support of UN sanctions against Iraq during Operation Southern Watch. (U.S. Navy / Erik Kenney)

Crash and Salvage personnel move into position for flight quarters on the flight deck of the USS *Theodore Roosevelt* (CVN 71) and its embarked Carrier Air Wing Eight (CVW-8) during a training mission in the Atlantic Ocean on 16 January 2003. (U.S. Navy / James K. McNeil)

Flight deck personnel aboard the Nimitz-class aircraft carrier USS *Harry S. Truman* (CVN 75) conduct aircraft salvage training with the emergency heavy lift crane, nicknamed "Tilly," while underway in the Arabian Gulf on 4 February 2005. An SH-60F Seahawk, assigned to the "Dusty Dogs" of Helicopter Anti-Submarine Squadron Seven (HS-7), was used as a mock crashed aircraft in the drill. Crash and Salvage crews often run drills simulating various kinds of accidents in order to improve their skill in fire-fighting and salvage operations. The *Truman* Carrier Strike Group is on a regularly scheduled deployment in support of the Global War on Terrorism. (U.S. Navy / Gregory A. Pierot)

During a mass casualty drill held on flight deck aboard USS *Carl Vinson* (CVN 70) on 3 June 2004, two crewman advance toward an aircraft fire to inspect a mock aircraft crash site after the fire has been contained. *Vinson* departed her homeport of Bremerton, Washington, for the coast of Southern California to reunite with Carrier Air Wing Nine (CVW-9) and conduct their next phase of readiness training in preparation for an upcoming deployment. (U.S. Navy / Refugio Carrillo)

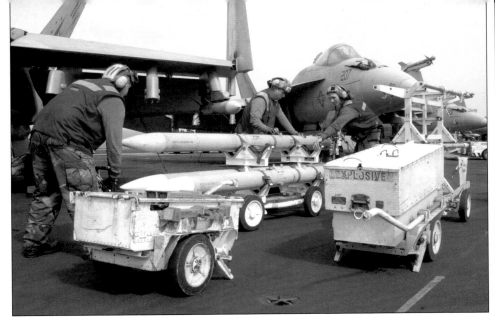

Aviation Ordnancemen assigned to the "Eagles" of Strike Fighter Squadron One One Five (VFA-115) move Advanced Medium Range Air to Air Missiles (AMRAAM) to F/A-18E "Super Hornets" in preparation for takeoff on 11 February 2003. (U.S. Navy / Tyler Clements)

An Aero 21A weapons skid supports a transporter unit drum on the deck of the nuclear-powered aircraft carrier USS *Dwight D. Eisenhower* (CVN 69) on 2 October 1987. The *Eisenhower* is participating in a week of carrier qualifications testing off the Virginia Capes. (U.S. Navy)

A flight deck crewman sits on the drawbar of a NAN-2 nitrogen servicing unit on the carrier USS *Dwight D. Eisenhower* (CVN-69) The NAN-2 is a portable unit for inflating or servicing aircraft tires on the hangar or flight deck. (U.S. Navy)

MD-3A tow tractors stand by on the flight deck of the nuclear-powered aircraft carrier USS *Carl Vinson* (CVN 70) prior to a barricade rigging and fire fighting drill on 4 October 1985. (U.S. Navy)

F/A-18F Super Hornets, assigned to the "Bounty Hunters" of Strike Fighter Squadron Two (VFA-2), prepare to launch from the flight deck aboard the USS *Abraham Lincoln* (CVN 72) on 14 July 2005. VFA-2 is assigned to Carrier Air Wing Two (CVW-2) embarked aboard the Nimitz-class aircraft carrier. *Lincoln* is at sea conducting readiness training in support of the Navy's Fleet Response Plan. (U.S. Navy / John Ivancic)

An F/A-18B Hornet, assigned to the "Fighting Omars" of Fighter Composite Squadron Twelve (VFC-12), prepares to make an arrested landing on the flight deck of the Nimitz-class aircraft carrier USS *Ronald Reagan* (CVN 76) on 11 August 2005. VFC-12 is the Naval Reserve's premier adversary squadron, providing threat-tactics-training to all Navy fighter and strike-fighter squadrons. *Reagan* was underway in the Pacific Ocean conducting carrier qualifications for the West Coast Fleet Replacement Squadrons. (U.S. Navy / Mahlon K. Miller)

The U.S. Navy's newest Strike Fighter, the F/A-18F Super Hornet, taxis towards a catapult aboard the Navy's newest nuclear powered aircraft carrier USS *John C. Stennis* (CVN 74) at the successful completion of sea trials on 23 January 1997. (U.S. Navy / Thomas M. Hensley)

A Fighter Squadron 143 (VF-143) F-14A Tomcat aircraft clears the leading edge of the angled flight deck of the nuclear-powered aircraft carrier USS *Dwight D. Eisenhower* (CVN 69), after being launched from the No. 4 waist catapult on 27 March 1990. (U.S. Navy)

An F-14D "Tomcat" from the "Tomcatters" of Fighter Squadron Three One (VF-31) flies over the Landing Signal Officer (LSO) platform aboard USS *Abraham Lincoln* (CVN 72) after returning from a successful proficiency flight on 26 January 2001. The *Lincoln* is in the Arabian Gulf in support of Operation Southern Watch. (U.S. Navy / Daniel Wolsey)

Air Department personnel watch as final checkers, assigned to the "Swordsmen" of Fighter Squadron Three Two (VF-32), inspect their F-14B Tomcat as it lines up along a steam-powered waist catapult prior to launching from the Nimitz-class aircraft carrier USS *Harry S. Truman* (CVN 75) during cyclic flight operations on 15 July 2005. *Truman* was conducting carrier qualifications and operations off the East Coast and was also participating in a Joint Task Force Exercise (JTFEX) with USS *Theodore Roosevelt* (CVN 71). JTFEX is a key component in the training cycle of an aircraft carrier and carrier air wing in the U.S. Navy Fleet Response Plan. (U.S. Navy / Kristopher Wilson)

An F/A-18C Hornet assigned to Marine Fighter Attack Training Squadron One Zero One (VMFAT-101), prepares to launch off the flight deck of the Nimitz-class carrier USS *Ronald Reagan* (CVN 76) on 13 December 2004. *Reagan* is conducting carrier qualifications for the West Coast fleet replacement squadrons. (U.S. Navy / Aaron Burden)

An F/A-18C Hornet from Strike Fighter Squadron 147 (VFA-147) "Argonauts," Naval Air Station (NAS) Lemoore, California, simulates a landing approach to the carrier USS *Nimitz* (CVN 68) on 16 September 1996, ported at North Island, California. The Hornet is armed with AIM-9 Sidewinders and AGM-65 Mavericks. (U.S. Navy)

A U.S. Navy Aviation Structural Mechanic gives the ready signal to a VFA-41 USN F/A-18F Super Hornet before launch aboard the Aircraft Carrier USS *Nimitz* (CVN 68) on 29 July 2005. The *Nimitz* Strike Group was on a regularly scheduled deployment and is participating in Maritime Security Operations (MSO). (U.S. Navy)

Calm descends on the forward flight deck of the USS *Abraham Lincoln* (CVN 72) during a lull in Carrier Qualifications on 12 August 2007. The *Lincoln* is back from refit for an extended seven months at the Puget Sound Naval Ship Yard in Bremerton, Wshington. (James C. Goodall)

Landing Safety Officers (LSO) guide in a T-45 "Goshawk" for a landing aboard USS *Theodore Roosevelt* (CVN 71) on 17 August 2003. *Roosevelt* was conducting training in the Atlantic Ocean. (U.S. Navy / Todd M. Flint)

With the exception of the EA-6B Prowlers, every other aircraft in this early 1980s photo of the deck of the USS *Carl Vinson* (CVN 70) has been retired from the Navy inventory. (U.S. Navy)

A TA-4J Skyhawk aircraft from Training Squadron 7 (VT-7) is prepared for launching during flight operations aboard the nuclear-powered aircraft carrier USS *Carl Vinson* (CVN 70) on 20 April 1984. (U.S. Navy)

An RF-8G Crusader aircraft of Photo Reconnaissance Squadron Two-Zero-Six (VFP-206) is about to catch the arresting cable during a landing on board the nuclear-powered aircraft carrier USS *Dwight D. Eisenhower* (CVN-69) on 19 September 1985. (U.S. Navy)

USS *Abraham Lincoln* (CVN 72) has a wide assortment of antenna. (U.S. Navy)

The grille shaped antenna on USS *Abraham Lincoln* (CVN 72) is the 3D Air Search Radar. (U.S. Navy)

The SPS-67 is a short-range, two-dimensional, surface-search/navigation radar system that provides accurate surface and limited low-flyer detection and tracking. (U.S. Navy)

The SPS-49 air search radar antenna is seen mounted atop the lattice mast of the nuclear-powered aircraft carrier USS *Theodore Roosevelt* (CVN-71) on 12 January 1990. (U.S. Navy)

Two SPS-65 low altitude radar antennas for the Mark 91 Fire Control System are seen on the nuclear-powered aircraft carrier USS *Theodore Roosevelt* (CVN-71) on 12 January 1990.

The lattice mast is seen behind the island of the nuclear-powered aircraft carrier USS *Theodore Roosevelt* (CVN-71) on 12 January 1990. The lattice mast supports the SPS-49 air search radar antenna.

A Fire Controlman scrubs down a Phalanx Close In Weapons System (CWIS) during periodic maintenance on the weapon on 19 December 2002. Phalanx is the only deployed close-in weapon systems capable of performing its own search, detects, evaluation, track, engage, and kill assessments. Phalanx fires up to 4,500 rounds of 20mm shells per minute. *Harry S. Truman* is on regularly scheduled deployment. (U.S. Navy / Dustin Gates)

A Pre-Aimed Calibration (PAC) test-fire is conducted on a Close in Weapons System (CIWS) to check the gun's bore alignment on 20 February 2003. CIWS is primarily used for air defense against missile and aircraft threats. USS *Carl Vinson* (CVN 70) was conducting operations in the Pacific Ocean. (U.S. Navy / Nicole Carter)

Fire Controlman 3rd Class Jeremiah Thompson, of Benicia, California, checks the barrel fittings on one of four Close-In Weapons System Mark Fifteen (CIWS MK 15) systems aboard USS *Abraham Lincoln* (CVN 72) on 15 August 2002. Petty Officer Thompson is assigned to the Combat Systems Department aboard the *Lincoln*. The *Lincoln* and Carrier Air Wing Fourteen (CVW 14) are *en route* to the Arabian Gulf in support of Operation Enduring Freedom. (U.S. Navy / Philip A. McDaniel)

A RIM-7 NATO "Sea Sparrow" missile launches from aboard USS *Harry S. Truman* (CVN 75) on 4 September 2002. The *Truman* is participating in a Composite Unit Training Exercise (COMPTUEX) which is designed to ready the ship, its onboard airing, and other vessels in the carrier's battle group to function as one cohesive fighting force. (U.S. Navy / H. Dwain Willis)

Fire Controlmen load a RIM-7 NATO "Sea Sparrow" missile during a launcher upload evaluation aboard the Nimitz-class carrier USS *Abraham Lincoln* (CVN 72) on 31 October 2004. The RIM-7 "Sea Sparrow" is a medium-range, rapid-reaction, missile weapon system that provides the capability of destroying hostile aircraft, anti-ship missiles and surface missile platforms. (U.S. Navy / James R. McGury)

A Fire Controlman assists in loading a NATO RIM-7 "Sea Sparrow" missile aboard USS *George Washington* (CVN 73) on 26 January 2004. The Navy uses the RIM-7 "Sea Sparrow" aboard ships as a surface-to-air anti-missile defensive weapon. The Norfolk, Virginia-based nuclear powered aircraft carrier is on a routine scheduled deployment. (U.S. Navy / Andrew Morrow)

Aircraft Carriers USS *Ronald Reagan* (CVN 76), USS *Kitty Hawk* (CV 63), and USS *Abraham Lincoln* (CVN 72) sail in formation near Guam at the start of Exercise Valiant Shield 2006 on 18 June 2006. (U.S. Navy / Spike Call)

An EA-6A Intruder aircraft of Tactical Electronic Warfare Squadron Two-Zero-Nine (VAQ-209) lands on board the nuclear-powered aircraft carrier USS *Dwight D. Eisenhower* (CVN-69) on 19 September 1985. (U.S. Navy)

A French Navy Rafale M multi-role combat fighter from the French aircraft carrier *Charles De Gaulle* performs a touch-and-go landing aboard the Nimitz-class aircraft carrier USS *Dwight D. Eisenhower* (CVN 69), during the Multi-National Maritime Exercise (MNME) 05-1 on 25 May 2005. (U.S. Navy / Peter Carnicelli)

Carrier Air Wing One (CVW-1) Landing Signal Officers (LSO) evaluate an ES-3A Shadow landing aboard the aircraft carrier USS *George Washington* (CVN 73) on 17 February 1998. *George Washington* and CVW-1 are conducting operations in the Arabian Gulf in support of Operation Southern Watch. (U.S. Navy)

(Above) The U.S. Navy aircraft carrier USS *Theodore Roosevelt* (CVN 71) conducts a weapons on-load with the ammunition ship USS *Santa Barbara* (AE 28) in the waters off the Virginia-Carolina coast following her post deployment yard period at the Norfolk Naval Shipyard in Portsmouth, Virginia, on 20 December 1995. (U.S. Navy)

(Left) The entire aircraft carrier USS *Nimitz* (CVN 68) is seen from above on 28 June 2001. (U.S. Navy)

(Below) More than 50 aircraft are parked on the flight deck of the USS *Dwight D. Eisenhower* (CVN 69) on 22 August 1985. On the bow, members of the Marine detachment are standing in a formation outlining the carrier's hull number. What is amazing about this photo taken in August 1985, twenty years later, the only aircraft type on the Ike's flight deck that are still operational are the E-2C Hawkeyes. (U.S. Navy)

The starboard side of the superstructure and antennas of the nuclear-powered aircraft carrier USS *Nimitz* (CVN 68) was photographed on 1 October 1986. (U.S. Navy)

Maintenance crew members work on Helicopter Anti-submarine Squadron 17 (HS-17) SH-3 Sea King helicopters beside the island of the nuclear-powered aircraft carrier USS *Abraham Lincoln* (CVN-72) prior to the ship's departure from port on 25 September 1990. (U.S. Navy)

An F/A-18F Super Hornet of the "Black Knights" of Strike Fighter Squadron One Five Four (VFA-154), undergoes final checks before launch from the flight deck of the Nimitz-class carrier USS *Carl Vinson* (CVN 70) on 8 April 2005. (U.S. Navy / Dusty Howell)

The island structure aboard the nuclear-powered aircraft carrier USS *Abraham Lincoln* (CVN-72) was photographed from the ship's port quarter on 24 November 1989. (U.S. Navy)

Spectators welcome the aircraft carrier, USS *Abraham Lincoln* (CVN 72), to Pearl Harbor on its way home from a nine-month deployment connected with Operation Iraqi Freedom on 26 April 2003. (U.S. Navy / Joshua L. Pritekel)

The island structure aboard the nuclear-powered aircraft carrier USS *Abraham Lincoln* (CVN-72) is seen here from the ship's bow on 24 November 1989. (U.S. Navy)

The name sake for the class, the USS *Chester M. Nimitz* (CVN 68) heads out to sea on its initial shake-down cruise and sea trials after leaving the Northrop Grumman Ship Building facilities in Hampton Roads, Virginia, in March 1975. (Northrop Grumman Shipbuilding)

High above the flight deck aboard USS *Dwight D. Eisenhower* (CVN 69) an Electrician's Mate prepares to lower a tool bag while a second Electrician's Mate manages the line after successfully servicing the ship's whistle on 5 January 2004. The Carrier Strike Group (CSG) was deployed conducting missions in support of Operation Iraqi Freedom and the continued war on terrorism. (U.S. Navy / Lance H. Mayhew Jr.)

A young crewman cleans the window covering the Pilot Landing Air Television (PLAT) camera aboard USS *George Washington* (CVN 73) on 19 March 2004. The Norfolk, Virginia-based nuclear powered aircraft carrier is on a regularly-scheduled deployment in support of Operation Iraqi Freedom (OIF). (U.S. Navy / Rex Nelson)

Antennas line the starboard side of the nuclear-powered aircraft carrier USS *Nimitz* (CVN 68) on 1 October 1986. (U.S. Navy)

SPS-49 air search radar antenna is seen mounted atop the lattice mast aboard the nuclear-powered aircraft carrier USS *Abraham Lincoln* (CVN 72) on 14 August 1990. (U.S. Navy)

SPN-43A carrier-controlled approach (CCA) radar antenna appears aboard the nuclear-powered aircraft carrier USS *Abraham Lincoln* (CVN 72) in this photograph dated 14 August 1990. (U.S. Navy)

The Nimitz-class aircraft carrier USS *Carl Vinson* (CVN 70) prepares to moor at a pier in Aprila Harbor, Santa Rita, Guam, during a scheduled port call on 21 February 2005. *Carl Vinson* was on a scheduled deployment after which it would head to Norfolk, Virginia, to prepare for refueling and a complex overhaul. (U.S. Navy / Nathanael T. Miller)

The bulbous bow of the Nimitz Class Aircraft Carrier, USS *Nimitz* (CVN 68) stands out as the ship sits in the graving dock area of the dry dock facilities at the Puget Sound Navy Yard in Bremerton, Washington, on 1 January 2002. (PSNSY)

The rudder, struts, and propellers at the stern of the Nimitz Class Aircraft Carrier, USS *Nimitz* (CVN 68), are clearly visible as the ship sits in the graving dock area of the dry dock facilities at the Puget Sound Navy Yard in Bremerton, Washington, on 1 January 2002. (PSNSY)

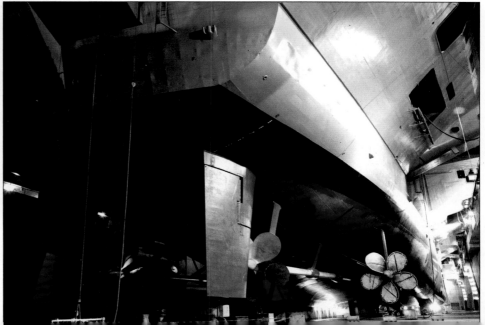

Puget Sound Naval Ship Yard workers from Bremerton, Washington, prepare the port side rudder of the USS *Abraham Lincoln* (CVN-72) for removal on 12 August 2003. *Lincoln* was undergoing a Planned Incremental Availability (PIA) at Puget Sound Naval Shipyard. (U.S. Navy / Derrick Eisenbeis)

Employees of Northrop Grumman shipyard install new propellers on USS *Carl Vinson* (CVN 70) in dry dock on 5 January 2007. The shaft and propeller project is a major milestone in the aircraft carrier's Refueling Complex Overhaul (RCOH). (U.S. Navy / Matthew Dewitt)

Workers from Northrop Grumman shipyard install a refurbished rudder on the Nimitz-class aircraft carrier USS *Carl Vinson* (CVN 70) in dry dock on 14 November 2006. (U.S. Navy / Tekeshia Affa)

Workers from Northrop Grumman shipyard install a refurbished rudder on USS *Carl Vinson* (CVN 70) on 14 November 2006. (U.S. Navy / Tekeshia Affa)

Workers from Northrop Grumman Shipbuilding check out a newly refurbished propeller shaft on the USS *Carl Vinson* (CVN 70) in dry dock in Newport News, Virginia, on 7 January 2007. The shaft and propeller project is a major milestone in the aircraft carrier's Refueling Complex Overhaul (RCOH) and is a final major component of outside-the-hull work before the ship's undocking in the fall of 2007. (U.S. Navy / Tekeshia Affa)

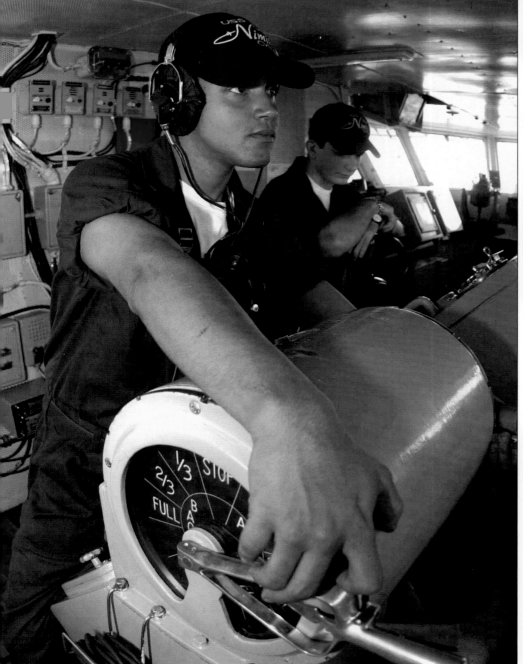

A Seaman Recruit pilots the USS *George Washington* (CVN 73) out of its port-o-call in Jabal 'Ali, Dubai, in the United Arab Emirates on 16 February 1998. *George Washington* was in the Arabian Gulf in support of Operation Southern Watch. (U.S. Navy)

U.S. Navy Boatswain's Mate aboard the USS *Theodore Roosevelt* (CVN 71), performs the duties of the lee helmsman while his shipmate, a U.S. Navy Boatswain's Mate does his portion of the work as the helmsman on 27 March 1999. The lee helmsman controls the ship's speed changes and the helmsman steers the ship. (U.S. Navy)

A Navy Seaman stands the lee helmsman watch in the Pilot House aboard USS *Nimitz* (CVN 68), deployed with its Carrier Air Wing Eleven (CVW-11) in the Western Pacific on 15 October 2003. (U.S. Navy / Yesenia Rosas)

An array of Gauges and switches line the helmsman's station on the bridge of the nuclear-powered aircraft carrier USS *Abraham Lincoln* (CVN-72) on 28 October 1990. (U.S. Navy)

A Boatswain's Mate of the Watch (BMOW) under instruction stands by to strike bells prior to being relieved from her watch on the bridge of the Nimitz-class Aircraft carrier USS *Ronald Reagan* (CVN 76) on 14 December 2004. Boatswain's Mate 3rd Class Nicole D. Goslin, of Eagle Point, Oregon, was qualifying to become the first female BMOW on board the *Reagan,* which was conducting carrier qualifications for the West Coast Fleet Replacement Squadrons in the Pacific. (U.S. Navy / Kitt A. Marchitnant)

A Quartermaster 3rd Class makes course corrections while steering the Nimitz-class aircraft carrier USS *Carl Vinson* (CVN 70) during an underway replenishment with the fast combat support ship USS *Camden* (AOE 2) on 11 March 2005. *Carl Vinson* was on a scheduled deployment, after which it would head to Norfolk, Virginia, to prepare for refueling and a complex overhaul. (U.S. Navy / Adan Fabela III)

Aviation Boatswain's Mate in Flight Deck Control marks the location of aircraft on the flight deck aboard USS *Abraham Lincoln* (CVN 72) on 29 October 2002. Lincoln and Carrier Air Wing Fourteen (CVW-14) were conducting combat missions in support of Operation Enduring Freedom and Southern Watch. (U.S. Navy / Tyler Clements)

Flight Deck Control personnel monitor flight operations while working alongside the "ouji board" in the Flight Deck Control Center aboard Nimitz-class aircraft carrier USS *Harry S. Truman* (CVN-75) on 11 December 2004. Carrier Air Wing Three (CVW-3), embarked aboard *Truman,* is providing close air support and conducting intelligence, surveillance, and reconnaissance (ISR) missions over Iraq. *Truman's* Carrier Strike Group Ten (CSG-10) and her embarked Carrier Air Wing Three (CVW-3) were on a regularly scheduled deployment in support of the Global War on Terrorism. (U.S. Navy / Kristopher Wilson)

An Aviation Boatswain's Mate keeps track of aircraft movement and maintenance status of Carrier Air Wing Three (CVW-3) on the "ouija board" in Hangar Bay Control on the nuclear-powered carrier USS *Harry S. Truman* (CVN 75), deployed in support of Operation Enduring Freedom, on 18 February 2003. (U.S. Navy / Danny Ewing Jr.)

Personnel stand watch in Air Operations (Air Ops), keeping track of air wing aircraft during flight operations aboard USS *Harry S. Truman* (CVN 75) on 9 April 2003. *Truman* and Carrier Air Wing Three (CVW-3) were deployed conducting combat missions in support of Operation Iraqi Freedom. (U.S. Navy / Andrea Decranini)

An Aviation Boatswain's Mate on Flight Deck Control marks the location of aircraft on the flight deck of the USS *Abraham Lincoln* (CVN 72) on 29 October 2002. *Lincoln* and Carrier Air Wing Fourteen (CVW-14) were on a regularly-scheduled six-month deployment conducting combat missions in support of Operation Enduring Freedom and Southern Watch. (U.S. Navy / Tyler Clements)

Operations Specialist 3rd uses the SPA-25 surface radar aboard USS *Abraham Lincoln* (CVN 72) to plot surface contacts on 26 October 2004. *Lincoln* and embarked Carrier Air Wing Two (CVW-2) were deployed to the Western Pacific Ocean. Carrier Strike Group Nine (CSG-9) is the first to be used in the surge role in support of the Chief of Naval Operations Fleet Response Plan. (U.S. Navy / Bernardo Fuller)

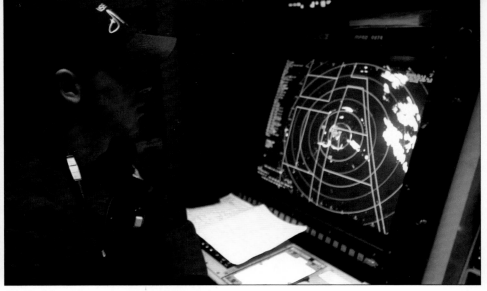

Two air traffic controllers stand watch at the 'Departure Control' console in the Carrier Control Approach (CCA) suite aboard USS *Harry S. Truman* (CVN 75) on 9 April 2003. *Truman* and Carrier Air Wing Three (CVW-3) were deployed conducting combat missions in support of Operation Iraqi Freedom. (U.S. Navy / Andrea Decemberanini)

Air Traffic Controllers man the Carrier Air Traffic Control Center (CATCC) during flight operations aboard USS *George Washington* (CVN 73) on 17 December 2003. The Norfolk, Virginia-based nuclear powered aircraft carrier is conducting Composite Training Unit Exercise (COMPTUEX) in the Atlantic Ocean, during preparations for an upcoming deployment. (U.S. Navy / Joan Kretschmer)

Air Traffic Controller 3rd Class stands as Case One Supervisor in Carrier Air Traffic Control Center (CATCC) during flight operations aboard the aircraft carrier USS *Nimitz* (CVN 68) on 9 November 2004. The Case One Supervisor is responsible for all personnel handling aircraft in CATCC during low visibility and night flight operations. *Nimitz* was conducting Tailored Ships Training Availability I/II/III and Final Exercise Problem off the coast of southern California. (U.S. Navy / Kristi Holmes)

Air Traffic Controllers stand watch in the Carrier Air Traffic Control Center (CATCC) aboard USS *George Washington* (CVN 73) on 24 March 2004. *George Washington* was deployed in support of Operation Iraqi Freedom (OIF). (U.S. Navy / Jessica Davis)

An officer uses the aircraft carrier's integrated shipboard information system on the USS *George Washington* (CVN 73) to monitor aircraft operating in the area while standing watch in the Carrier Air Traffic Control Center (CATCC) on 1 August 2002. USS *George Washington* (CVN 73) and Carrier Air Wing One Seven (CVW-17) were on a regularly-scheduled deployment, conducting combat missions in support of Operation Enduring Freedom. (U.S. Navy / Andrew Morrow)

NASCAR Nextel Cup driver John Andretti pays a visit to the Air Traffic Control crew in the Carrier Air Traffic Control Center (CATCC) aboard the Nimitz-class aircraft carrier USS *Harry S. Truman* (CVN 75) on 7 December 2004. Carrier Air Wing Three (CVW-3) embarked aboard *Truman* is providing close air support and conducting intelligence, surveillance and reconnaissance missions over Iraq. *Truman's* Carrier Strike Group Ten (CSG-10) and CVW-3 are on a regularly-scheduled deployment in support of the Global War on Terrorism. (U.S. Navy / Ricardo Reyes)

Air Traffic Controllers keep a watchful eye on their radar screens in the ship's Carrier Air Traffic Control Center (CATCC) on 29 January 2004. The personnel assigned to the CATCC monitor and direct aircraft within 50 numerical miles of the nuclear-powered aircraft carrier. (U.S. Navy / Lucious P. Alexander Jr)

A Naval Aviator assigned to the "Swordsmen" of Fighter Squadron Three Two (VF-32) dresses out in flight gear during preparations for combat mission over Iraq on 20 March 2003. The aircraft carrier USS *Harry S. Truman* (CVN 75) and Carrier Air Wing Three (CVW-3) were conducting missions in support of Operation Iraqi Freedom. (U.S. Navy / Christopher B. Stoltz)

U.S. Naval Aviators assigned to the "Checkmates" of Sea Control Squadron Two Two (VS-22) dress out in flight gear during preparations for a combat mission over Iraq on 21 March 2003. The aircraft carrier USS *Harry S. Truman* (CVN 75) and Carrier Air Wing Three (CVW-3) were on deployment conducting combat missions in support of Operation Iraqi Freedom. (U. S. Navy / Andrea Decemberanini)

Naval Aviators assigned to the "Swordsmen" of Fighter Squadron Three Two (VF-32) dress out in flight gear during preparations for combat mission over Iraq on 20 March 2003. (U.S. Navy / Christopher B. Stoltz)

Aviation Anti-Submarine Warfare officer receives help from Survival Equipment specialist with donning his chemical biological radiological (CBR) mask during a drill aboard USS *Abraham Lincoln* (CVN 72) on 23 March 2003. (U. S. Navy / Jeanine A. Garcia)

High above the flight deck, the "Mini Boss" watches a C-2A "Greyhound" land on the USS *Abraham Lincoln* (CVN 72) on 11 November 2002. The Mini Boss aboard any aircraft carrier operates from the ship's Primary Flight Control center, managing day-to-day flight operations on ship's flight deck, including the air space immediately around the carrier. *Abraham Lincoln* was conducting combat missions in support of Operations Southern Watch and Enduring Freedom. (U.S. Navy / Philip A. McDaniel)

The Interior Communications man aboard USS *Harry S. Truman* (CVN 75) mans the Pilot's Landing Aid Television (PLAT) camera, while his counterpart makes calls over the sound-powered phone on 12 September 2003. The carrier was in the Atlantic Ocean, completing its Comprehensive Training Unit Exercise (COMPTUEX), in preparation for deployment to the Mediterranean Sea. (U.S. Navy / Lance H. Mayhew Jr)

A Quartermaster monitors an SPA-25-G radar console on the navigational bridge of the USS *George Washington* (CVN 73) on 27 June 2002. The carrier is on a regularly-scheduled six-month deployment conducting missions in support of Operation Enduring Freedom. (U.S. Navy / Andrew Morrow)

An Operations Specialist tracks surface contacts in the Tactical Operation Plot (TOP) on the bridge aboard the Nimitz-class aircraft carrier USS *Harry S. Truman* (CVN 75) on 18 November 2004. Truman's Carrier Strike Group Ten (CSG-10) and her embarked Carrier Airwing Three (CVW-3) were on a scheduled deployment in support of the Global War on Terrorism. (U.S. Navy / Danny Ewing Jr)

A Sailor aboard USS *Harry S. Truman* (CVN 75) searches for potential threats during his watch in the Combat Direction Center (CDC), where the aircraft carrier monitors all surface and air contacts in the ship's vicinity. On 20 March 2003 *Truman* was deployed in support of Operation Iraqi Freedom. (U.S. Navy / H. Dwain Willis)

An Operations Specialist (left) tracks interceptions of aircraft and reports them to the Tactical Actions Officer (TAO), (right) in the Combat Direction Center (CDC) on 25 November 2003. The CDC, the nerve center of the nuclear-powered USS *Harry S. Truman* (CVN 75), is where information is collected, processed, displayed, evaluated, and disseminated from sources outside and inside the ship. (U.S. Navy / Rob Gaston)

An Operations Specialist tracks interceptions of aircraft and controls schedules for flight operations using the status board in the Combat Direction Center (CDC) of the USS *Harry S. Truman* (CVN 75), on 25 November 2003. The nerve center of the vessel, the CDC is where information from sources inside and outside the ship is collected, processed, displayed, evaluated, and disseminated. (U.S. Navy / Rob Gaston)

The Tactical Actions Officer (TAO) stands watch in the Combat Direction Center (CDC) aboard USS *Harry S. Truman* (CVN 75) on 10 April 2003. *Truman* and Carrier Air Wing Three (CVW-3) were deployed conducting combat missions in support of Operation Iraqi Freedom. (U.S. Navy / Christopher B. Stoltz)

Deputy Carrier Airwing Commander (DCAG) for Carrier Airwing Three (CVW-3), second from left, receives input from a member of Seal Team Eight as well as pilots from several squadrons within CVW-3 during a brief in the Mission Planning room aboard USS *Harry S. Truman* (CVN 75) on 19 March 2003. *Truman* and CVW-3 were deployed conducting missions in support of Operation Iraqi Freedom. (U.S. Navy / Michael W. Pendergrass)

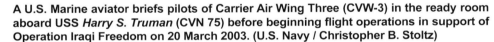

A U.S. Marine aviator briefs pilots of Carrier Air Wing Three (CVW-3) in the ready room aboard USS *Harry S. Truman* (CVN 75) before beginning flight operations in support of Operation Iraqi Freedom on 20 March 2003. (U.S. Navy / Christopher B. Stoltz)

A lieutenant commander attached to the "Checkmates" of Sea Control Squadron Two Two (VS-22) briefs pilots in squadron ready room 4 aboard the aircraft carrier USS *Harry S. Truman* (CVN 75) on 12 March 2003. Pilots were preparing to participate in a scheduled War At Sea Exercise (WASEX) training flight crewmembers for a coordinated attack on a deployed enemy vessel. (U. S. Navy / Michael W. Pendergrass)

Minutes after landing an F-14 Tomcat fighter aircraft aboard USS *Harry S. Truman* (CVN 75), the flight crew is debriefed in the Carrier Intelligence Center (CVIC) on 20 March 2003, during Operation Iraqi Freedom. (U.S. Navy / Michael W. Pendergrass)

An Aviation Boatswain's Mate mans an arresting gear machinery room under the flight deck aboard the aircraft carrier USS *Abraham Lincoln* (CVN 72) on 28 March 2003. The Petty Officer varies the resistance of the number arresting wires on the ship's flight deck depending on the weight and type of aircraft being recovered as well as monitoring operating pressures. *Lincoln* and Carrier Air Wing 14 (CVW 14) were conducting combat operations in support of Operation Iraqi Freedom. (U.S. Navy / Jason Frost)

An Aviation Boatswain's Mate adjusts the tension of arresting gear machinery under the flight deck aboard USS *John C. Stennis* (CVN 74) on 13 August 2003. *Stennis* was at sea conducting training exercises in the Southern California operating area. (U.S. Navy / Mark J. Rebilas)

An Airman adjusts the arresting gear machinery according to the weight of the approaching aircraft to create proper tension when the arresting wire is caught by the tailhook. The USS Abraham Lincoln (CVN 72) and Carrier Air Wing One Four (CVW-14) were conducting combat operations in support of Operation Southern Watch on 6 March 2003. (U.S. Navy / Bernardo Fuller)

An Aviation Boatswain's Mate conducts a visual inspection of his equipment while standing the Number One Arresting Gear Engine Watch as flight operations are conducted aboard the Nimitz-class aircraft carrier USS *Ronald Reagan* (CVN 76) on 28 June 2005. The Nimitz-class nuclear powered aircraft carrier was underway conducting carrier qualifications. (U.S. Navy / Aaron Burden)

Hull Maintenance Technician Fireman and Boatswains assigned to USS *Harry S. Truman* (CVN 75), prepare to fight a simulated fire during a General Quarters (GQ) drill on 24 June 2004. Enterprise was one of seven carriers participating in Summer Pulse 2004, a simultaneous deployment of seven aircraft carrier strike groups (CSGs), demonstrating the ability of the Navy to provide credible combat power across the globe, in five theaters with other U.S., allied, and coalition military forces. Summer Pulse was the Navy's first deployment under its new Fleet Response Plan (FRP). (U.S. Navy / Alex J. Recalde)

An Aviation Boatswain's Mate operates the fuel console in an aviation fuel pump control room on 18 February 2002. The USS *John C. Stennis* (CVN 74) and Carrier Air Wing Nine (CVW-9) were deployed in support of Operation Enduring Freedom. (U.S. Navy / Joshua Word)

A Machinist Mate assigned to the O2/N2 Plant aboard aircraft carrier USS *Abraham Lincoln* (CVN 72), fills a liquid oxygen cart with -297 degree Fahrenheit liquid oxygen before transporting it to a jet to supply aviators with breathing oxygen at high elevations on 13 August 2004. *Lincoln* was conducting operations in preparation for deployment. (U.S. Navy / Bernardo Fuller)

An Aviation Boatswain runs the controls for a steam-powered catapult as he communicates with a phone talker on the flight deck aboard the Nimitz-class aircraft carrier USS *Abraham Lincoln* (CVN 72) on 21 January 2005. The *Abraham Lincoln* Carrier Strike group was operating in the Indian Ocean off the coasts of Indonesia and Thailand in support of Operation Unified Assistance, the humanitarian operation effort in the wake of the tsunami that struck South East Asia. (U.S. Navy / Cristina R. Morrison)

A Deck Department Sailor stationed aboard the Nimitz-class aircraft carrier USS *Dwight D. Eisenhower* (CVN 69) monitors a fuel hose as it is pulled into the connector during a replenishment at sea with the Military Sealift Command (MSC) fast combat support ship USNS *Arctic* (T-AOE 8) on 5 May 2006. *Eisenhower* and embarked Carrier Air Wing Seven (CVW-7) were participating in their Unit Exercise (COMPTUEX). (U.S. Navy / Christopher B. Long)

The Nimitz-class aircraft carrier USS *Theodore Roosevelt* (CVN 71) performs a connected replenishment with the Military Sealift Command (MSC) underway replenishment oilier USNS *Kanawha* (T-AO 196) in the Atlantic Ocean on 10 August 2005. *Roosevelt* and embarked Carrier Air Wing Eight (CVW-8) were underway on a regularly-scheduled deployment in support of the Global War on Terrorism. (U.S. Navy / Randall Damm)

Sailors aboard the nuclear powered aircraft carrier USS *Nimitz* (CVN 68) monitor refueling hoses from the Military Sealift Command (MSC) underway replenishment oilier USNS *Walter S. Diehl* (T-AO 193) during a replenishment at sea on 16 November 2005. The *Nimitz* and embarked Carrier Air Wing Eleven (CVW-11) were conducting operations in the Western Pacific Ocean. (U.S. Navy / Patrick L. Heil)

USS *Harry S. Truman* (CVN 75) Deck Department Sailors spray off the anchor with fire hoses as the ship prepares to get underway with Carrier Air Wing Three (CVW-3) on 4 February 2003. *Truman* completed a port call in Koper, Slovenia, during deployment in support of Operation Enduring Freedom. (U.S. Navy / Derrick M. Snyder)

USS *Carl Vinson* (CVN 70) Deck Department's 1st Division conducts a precision anchoring drill under the direction of the Ship's Boatswain on 3 May 2004. During this exercise the Deck Department is graded on its ability to drop anchor on a pre-designated coordinate. It is one of many exercises that the Bremerton, Washington- based aircraft carrier underwent during a Tailored Ships Training Availability (TSTA). (U.S Navy / Nicole Carter)

An Aviation Structural Mechanic and a Ship's Serviceman, prime the ship's Anchor after notification that the coveted Golden Anchor Award was being awarded on 16 January 2004. (U.S. Navy / Lucious P. Alexander Jr)

Squadron personnel perform maintenance on F/A-18 Hornets parked in the hangar bay of the Nimitz-class aircraft carrier USS *Harry S. Truman* (CVN 75) 27 October 2004. Truman was participating in the Joint Maritime Course, a multinational NATO exercise off the coast of Scotland. (U.S. Navy / Jomo K. Coffea)

Sailors assigned to the "Swordsman" of Fighter Squadron Thirty Two (VF-32) perform maintenance on an F-14 Tomcat in the hangar bay after it had broken the sound barrier during an air power demonstration 28 April 2003. USS *Harry S. Truman* (CVN 75) and Carrier Air Wing Three (CVW-3) were on deployment conducting missions in support of Operation Iraqi Freedom. (U.S. Navy / Ryan O'Connor)

Most of the aircraft types that are seen here filling the hangar of the nuclear-powered aircraft carrier USS *Dwight D. Eisenhower* (CVN 69) on 13 April 1987 would no longer be in the active Navy inventory by the end of the first decade of the 21st Century. (U.S. Navy)

These A-7B Corsair II aircraft in the hangar bay of the nuclear-powered aircraft carrier USS *Carl Vinson* (CVN 70) on 15 June 1982 were assigned to Light Attack Squadrons 203, 204, and 205 (VA-203, 204, 205). (U.S. Navy / Dan McGrath)

A sailor pulls out the refueling probe from an Aerial Refueling Store (ARS) during maintenance in the hangar bay aboard the Nimitz-class aircraft carrier USS *Carl Vinson* (CVN 70) on 27 March 1989. The Aerial Refueling Store (ARS) is a combination external fuel tank and hose reel used for aerial refueling operations. *Carl Vinson* ended its deployment with a homeport shift to Norfolk, Virginia. (U.S. Navy / Joshua Hammond)

An F/A-18F Super Hornet, assigned to the "Bounty Hunters" of Strike Fighter Squadron Two (VFA-2), is prepared to do an engine run up after the replacement of its General Electric F-414 on 11 August 2007. VFA-2 was assigned to Carrier Air Wing Two (CVW-2), which was embarked aboard the Nimitz-class aircraft carrier, *Lincoln,* which was at sea conducting readiness training in support of the Navy's Fleet Response Plan. (James C. Goodall)

Sailors from the "Black Aces" of Strike Fighter Squadron Four One (VFA-41) aboard the USS *Nimitz* (CVN 68), move a Shared Reconnaissance Pod (SHARP) from the ship's hangar bay to the Aircraft Intermediate Maintenance Department (AIMD) jet shop to perform operational checks on 11 January 2003. *Nimitz* was on a Composite Unit Training Exercise (COMTUEX) off the coast of San Diego, California. (U.S. Navy / Tiffini M. Jones)

Sailors assigned to the "Swordsmen" of Fighter Squadron Thirty Two (VF-32) perform maintenance on an F-14 Tomcat in the hangar bay aboard USS *Harry S. Truman* (CVN 75) on 28 April 2003. Truman and Carrier Air Wing Three (CVW-3) were on deployment conducting missions in support of Operation Iraqi Freedom. (U.S. Navy / Ryan O'Connor)

Aviation Machinist's Mates assigned to the Aircraft Intermediate Maintenance Department's jet shop aboard USS *George Washington* (CVN 73) receive data while testing a jet engine after repair on 24 January 2004. (U.S. Navy / Joan Kretschmer)

An Aviation Machinist's Mate tests an F110-GE400 jet engine prior to installation in an F-14 Tomcat aboard USS *George Washington* (CVN 73) on 20 November 2003. (U.S. Navy / Janice Kreischer)

An F404-GE-402 engine for an F/A-18 Hornet is tested on the fantail aboard Nimitz-class aircraft carrier USS *Abraham Lincoln* (CVN 72) on 23 June 2004. *Lincoln* was conducting local operations in preparation for an upcoming scheduled deployment, after 10 months of dry docked Planned Incremental Availability (PIA). (U.S. Navy / Jeremie M. Yode)

An EA-6B Prowler aircraft engine glows during testing at the Aviation Intermediate Maintenance Department's (AIMD) jet engine test cell aboard USS *Ronald Reagan* (CVN 76) on 1 December 2004. The nuclear-powered aircraft carrier was underway in the Pacific Ocean conducting routine carrier operations. (U.S. Navy / Chad McNeeley)

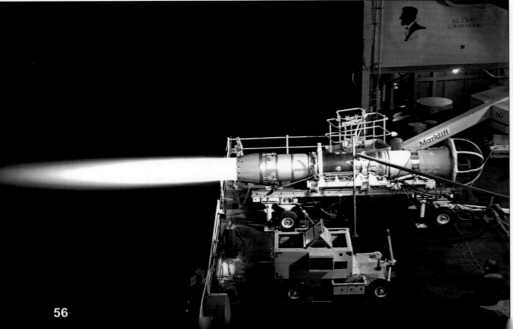

Two Aviation Machinist Mates prepare a General Electric F-110 series jet engine for testing in the engine shop aboard USS *George Washington* (CVN 73) on 11 December 2003. The Norfolk, Virginia-based nuclear powered aircraft carrier was conducting Composite Training Unit Exercises (COMPTUEX) in preparation for an upcoming six-month deployment. (U.S. Navy / Michael D. Blackwell)

Personnel from the Aircraft Intermediate Maintenance Department (AIMD) prepare to place a jet engine onto an installation trailer aboard USS *Nimitz* (CVN 68) on 4 January 2004. The *Nimitz* Carrier Strike Group (CSG) was deployed in support of Operation Iraqi Freedom and the continued war on terrorism. (U.S. Navy / Lucious Alexander)

An Aviation Machinist's Mate uses an overhead winch to position a High Pressure Compressor, from a GE-414 Jet Engine, to be put into its shipping container so that it can be preserved for shipping back to the manufacturer on 9 February 2003. (U.S. Navy / Daniel C. Johnson)

A USS *Abraham Lincoln* (CVN 72) Aviation Machinist's Mate prepares to use a torque wrench while conducting maintenance on a F404-GE-402 jet engine in preparation for testing on 4 June 2004. *Lincoln* spent ten and a half months in dry dock for the ship's Planned Incremental Availability (PIA) and was conducting local operations in preparation for deployment in the following year. (U.S. Navy / Michael S. Kelly)

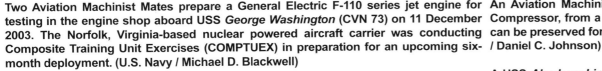

57

An F/A-18 "Hornet" launches from the flight deck of the USS *John C. Stennis* (CVN 74) on 22 March 2002. *Stennis* and Carrier Air Wing Nine (CVW-9) were conducting combat missions in support of Operation Enduring Freedom. (U.S. Navy / Jayme T. Pastoric)

USS *George Washington* (CVN 73) crewmembers assigned to the weapons department move ordnance from the flight deck to the hangar bay prior to final storage within the ship's weapons magazines on 29 June 2002. The ship, ported in Yokota, Japan, was on a regularly-scheduled six-month deployment conducting missions in support of Operation Enduring Freedom. (U.S. Navy / Jessica Davis)

An HH-60H Seahawk, assigned to the "Black Knights" of Helicopter Anti-Submarine Squadron Four (HS-4), prepares to land aboard USS *John C. Stennis* (CVN 74) on 21 October 2004. *Stennis* and embarked Carrier Air Wing Fourteen (CVW-14) are returning from a scheduled deployment to the Western Pacific Ocean. (U.S. Navy / Marchk J. Rebilas)

An F/A-18 Hornet from the "Salty Dogs" of Air Test and Evaluation Squadron Two Three (VX-23) makes the first arrested landing or "trap" on the flight deck of the carrier USS *Ronald Reagan* (CVN 76) on 24 July 2003. (U.S. Navy / Chad McNeeley)

Crew members gather around two A-7E Corsair IIs and a French Marine F-8E (FN) Crusader aircraft aboard the nuclear-powered aircraft carrier USS *Dwight D. Eisenhower* (CVN-69) on 21 May 1983. (U.S. Navy)

A British Royal Navy FRS.Mk 1 Sea Harrier aircraft taxis on the flight deck after landing aboard the nuclear-powered aircraft carrier USS *Dwight D. Eisenhower* (CVN 69) on 22 October 1984. (U.S. Navy)

An Argentine navy S-2E Tracker aircraft lands on the flight deck of the nuclear-powered aircraft carrier USS *Abraham Lincoln* (CVN-72) on 23 October 1990. The aircraft was taking part in touch-and-go operations aboard the *Lincoln* during the ship's circumnavigation of South America. (U.S. Navy / Don Montgomery)

A Super Etendard aircraft of the Argentine navy prepares to land on the flight deck of the USS *Abraham Lincoln* (CVN-72) on 23 October 1990. (U.S. Navy / Don Montgomery)

Weapons department personnel restow a MK-82 500 pound bomb in one of the ship's weapons magazines aboard USS *George Washington* (CVN 73) on 7 August 2002. The Washington battle group was on a regularly scheduled deployment conducting missions in support of Operation Enduring Freedom. (U.S. Navy / Corey T. Lewis)

Aviation Ordnancemen transfer ordnance through the mess deck elevators *en route* to the flight deck aboard USS *Harry S. Truman* (CVN 75) for use in missions over Iraq on 22 March 2003. *Truman* was deployed in support of Operation Iraqi Freedom. (U.S. Navy / Andrea Decanini)

Aviation Ordnancemen from the USS *George Washington* (CVN 73) remove a bomb stabilizing unit from a Mark 82 500-pound bomb in one of the ship's weapons magazines on 7 August 2002. The *Washington* battle group was on a six-month deployment conducting missions in support of Operation Enduring Freedom. (U.S. Navy / Corey T. Lewis)

An Aviation Ordnanceman installs an FMU-139BB "electric tail fuse" on a 500-pound BLU-111 Penetrating bomb while working in one of the weapons magazines aboard the USS *John C. Stennis* (CVN 74) on 5 March 2002. *Stennis* and Carrier Air Wing Nine (CVW-9) were conducting combat missions in support of Operation Enduring Freedom. (U.S. Navy / James A. Farrally II)

Aviation Ordnancemen transfer ordnance through the mess deck elevators en route to the flight deck aboard USS *Harry S. Truman* (CVN 75) for use in missions over Iraq on 22 March 2003. Truman was deployed in support of Operation Iraqi Freedom. (U.S. Navy / Photographer's Mate 2nd Class Andrea Decanini)

Joint Direct Attack Munitions (JDAM) sit on the mess deck in temporary storage prior to being moved to the flight deck to be loaded onto awaiting air wing aircraft on 20 March 2003. The aircraft carrier USS *Abraham Lincoln* (CVN 72) and Carrier Air Wing Fourteen (CVW-14) were conducting combat operations in support of Operation Iraqi Freedom. (U.S. Navy / Michael S. Kelly)

Ordnance is transported via weapons elevator from the ship's hangar bay to weapons magazines below decks aboard the aircraft carrier USS *Harry S. Truman* (CVN 75) on 1 May 2004. *Truman* was undergoing her Tailored Ship's Training Availability (TSTA) exercise off the Atlantic Coast. (U.S. Navy / John L. Beeman)

61

Boatswain's Mate, a search and rescue (SAR) swimmer assigned to the Nimitz-class aircraft carrier USS *Theodore Roosevelt* (CVN 71) stands aboard a Rigid Hull Inflatable Boat (RHIB) after a simulated search and rescue drill on 16 May 2006. *Roosevelt* was underway conducting qualifications as part of the fleet response plan. (U.S. Navy / Chris Thamann)

Crewmembers assigned to the Deck Department lower a Rigid Hull Inflatable Boat (RHIB) during a man-overboard drill aboard the guided missile cruiser USS *Vella Gulf* (CG 72) on 20 April 2004. *Vella Gulf* is assigned to the USS *George Washington* (CVN 73) Carrier Strike Group (CSG). The Norfolk, Virginia-based cruiser was on a regular deployment in support of Operation Iraqi Freedom (OIF). (U.S. Navy / Rex Nelson)

Chief Boatswain's Mate instructs Deck Department personnel on deploying a rigid-hull inflatable (RHIB) boat for man-overboard situations aboard the Nimitz-class aircraft carrier USS *Theodore Roosevelt* (CVN 71) on 7 January 2005. *Roosevelt* and embarked Carrier Air Wing Eight (CVW-8) were underway on a regularly scheduled deployment conducting Maritime security operations. (U.S. Navy / Nathan Laird)

On 15 June 2005, the Nimitz-class aircraft carrier USS *Ronald Reagan* (CVN 76) activates its countermeasures washdown system as part of a series of test and evaluations to certify the vessel in the event of a chemical, biological, or radiological attack. The sprinkler system also provides protection against flight deck fires. *Reagan* was underway in the Pacific Ocean conducting a Board of Inspection and Survey inspection. (U.S. Navy / John S. Lill)

At sea aboard Precommissioning Unit (PCU) *Ronald Reagan* (CVN 76) Damage Controlmen inspect the ship's hangar bay damage control sprinkler systems during functional tests at sea on 7 May 2003. *Reagan* was conducting a scheduled ship builder sea trial off the coast of Virginia. *Ronald Reagan* joined the fleet during commissioning ceremonies on 12 July 2003. (U.S. Navy / Rusty Black)

A periodic test of the Aqueous Film Forming Foam (AFFF) and countermeasure washdown sprinkler system is underway on the flight deck of the USS *Harry S. Truman* (CVN 75) on 29 January 2003. The sprinkler system is a vital feature during emergency circumstances requiring aircraft fire fighting or protection against harmful airborne contaminants. The *Truman* was conducting sea trials after completing a seven-month Planned Incremental Availability (PIA) period. (U.S. Navy / Jayme Pastoric)

USS *Nimitz* (CVN 68), and USS *Ronald Reagan* (CVN 76) navigate alongside each other during routine training exercises off the southern California coast on 16 November 2004. (U.S. Navy / Elizabeth Thompson)

The Nimitz-class aircraft carrier USS *Abraham Lincoln* (CVN 72) arrives in Pearl Harbor, Hawaii, on 23 February 2005, after deployment to the Western Pacific in support of Operation Unified Assistance, the humanitarian relief effort to aid the victims of the tsunami that struck Southeast Asia. (U.S. Navy / Dennis C. Cantrell)

The USS *Carl Vinson* (CVN 70) and fast combat support ship USS *Sacramento* (AOE 1) engage in an underway replenishment (UNREPS) during extended deployment in the Western Pacific on 16 August 2003. UNREPS are regularly scheduled evolutions for replenishing food stores, materials, and fuel. (U.S. Navy / Jonathan M. Cirino)

A B-2 Stealth Bomber assigned to Whiteman Air Force Base (AFB), Missouri, leads an aerial flight formation during Exercise Valiant Shield 2006. The *Abraham Lincoln* Carrier Strike group was participating in Exercise Valiant Shield along with the *Ronald Reagan* Carrier Strike Group and the *Kitty Hawk* Carrier Strike Group on 18 June 2006. Valiant Shield focused on integrated joint training among U.S. military forces, enabling real-world proficiency in sustaining joint forces and in detecting, locating, tracking, and engaging units at sea, in the air, on land, and cyberspace in response to a range of mission areas. (U.S. Navy)

After a port call in Singapore, the Nimitz-class aircraft carrier USS *Ronald Reagan* (CVN 76) transits the Bay of Bengal on 12 February 2006. *Reagan* was on its maiden deployment in support of the global war on terrorism and maritime security operations (MSO). (U.S. Navy / Christopher Brown)

The Nimitz-class aircraft carrier USS *John C. Stennis* (CVN 74) transits through the Pacific Ocean on 14 March 2006. *Stennis* was conducting carrier qualifications off the coast of Southern California. (U.S. Navy / Paul J. Perkins)

USS *Harry S. Truman* (CVN-75) steams underway in the Eastern Mediterranean Sea on 29 March 2003. Truman was deployed in support of Operation Iraqi Freedom. (U.S. Navy / Michael W. Pendergrass)

The aircraft carrier USS *George Washington* (CVN 73) is conducting an ammunition transfer with the USS *Harry S. Truman* (CVN 75) (not pictured) on 13 September 2004. Carrier qualifications were going on at the time off the East Coast of the United States. (U.S. Navy / Ryan T. O'Connor)

Following a four-day port visit to Greece's largest island, USS *Harry S. Truman* (CVN 75) sails out of Souda harbor in Crete on 8 November 2004. *Truman* and embarked Carrier Air Wing Three (CVW-3) were on a regularly-scheduled deployment in support of the Global War on Terrorism. (U.S. Navy / Paul Farley)

In the harbor at Naval Station, Subic Bay, in the Philippines, the large harbor tugs *Kalispell* (YTB 784) and *Wauwatosa* (YTB 774) assist at the stern as USS *Carl Vinson* (CVN 70) is maneuvered into a dock on 24 December 1984. (U.S. Navy)

F-14D Tomcats launch from the flight deck of USS *Theodore Roosevelt* (CVN 71) to their homeport of Naval Air Station Oceana on 10 March 2006. VF-213 and VF-31 were completing their final deployment flying the F-14 Tomcat. (U.S. Navy / Chris Thamann)

The Nimitz-class aircraft carrier USS *Dwight D. Eisenhower* (CVN 69) gets under way from Pier 12 on board Naval Station Norfolk on 18 October 2005. *Eisenhower* completed a three-year refueling and complex overhaul in March and this was her first under way period since completing the repairs. (U.S. Navy / Laura A. Moore)

The Nimitz-class aircraft carrier USS *Dwight D. Eisenhower* (CVN 69). *Eisenhower* is underway participating in the Joint Task Force Exercise (JTFEX) Operations Bold Step, an exercise involving more than 16,000 service members from five countries on 28 Jully 2006. (Miguel Angel Contreras / U.S. Navy)

The Nimitz-class aircraft carrier USS *Carl Vinson* (CVN 70) transits through the Strait of Gibraltar *en route* to the Atlantic Ocean on 19 July 2005. *Carl Vinson* will end its deployment with a homeport shift from San Diego, California to Norfolk, Virginia, and commence a three-year refuel and complex overhaul. (Chris M. Valdez / U.S. Navy)

The Nimitz-class aircraft carrier USS *Abraham Lincoln* (CVN 72) operates off the coast of Banda Aceh, Sumatra, Indonesia on 7 January 2005. Helicopters assigned to Carrier Air Wing Two (CVW-2) and Sailors from *Abraham Lincoln* are supporting Operation Unified Assistance, the humanitarian operation effort in the wake of the tsunami that struck South East Asia. The *Abraham Lincoln* Carrier Strike Group was operating in the Indian Ocean off the waters of Indonesia and Thailand. (Seth C. Peterson / U.S. Navy)

The Nimitz-class aircraft carrier USS *Harry S. Truman* (CVN) and her embarked Carrier Air Wing Three (CVW-3) steam through the Mediterranean Sea on their regularly scheduled deployment in support of Operation Enduring Freedom on 10 January 2003. (John L. Beeman / U.S. Navy)

The aircraft carrier USS *Nimitz* (CVN 68) is conducting a Composite Training Unit Exercise along the coast of southern California, on 11 December 2004. (U.S. Navy / Shannon E. Renfroe)

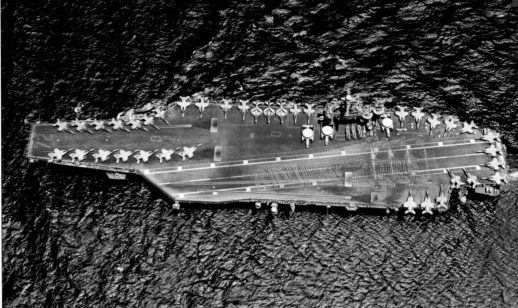

Following a seven-month maintenance period, USS John C. Stennis (CVN-74) conducts high-speed steering and maneuvering checks off the southern California coast on 20 April 2001. Such tests are necessary to ensure that all systems function properly in emergency situations as well as under routine conditions. (U.S. Navy / James A. Farrally II)

The Nimitz-class aircraft carrier USS *Harry S. Truman* is underway while on station in the Arabian Gulf on 8 February 2005. Carrier Air Wing Three (CVW-3) was embarked aboard *Truman*, providing close air support and conducting intelligence surveillance and reconnaissance over Iraq. The *Truman* Carrier Strike Group was on a regularly-scheduled deployment in support of the global war on terrorism. (U.S. Navy / Rome J Toledo)

Sailors aboard USS *Abraham Lincoln* (CVN 72) spell out "RIMPAC 2006" on the flight deck during a photo exercise on 25 July 2006. To commemorate the last day of RIMPAC, participating countries' naval vessels fell into ranks for a photo exercise. Eight nations participated in RIMPAC, the world's largest biennial maritime exercise. Conducted in the waters off Hawaii, RIMPAC brings together military forces from Australia, Canada, Chile, Peru, Japan, the Republic of Korea, the United Kingdom and the United States. (U.S. Navy / James R. Evans)

USS *Ronald Reagan* (CVN 76) conducts rudder checks as part of the ship's Board of Inspection and Survey (INSURV) following a six-month Planned Incremental Availability on 30 October 2007. All naval vessels are periodically inspected by INSURV to check their material condition and battle readiness. (U.S. Navy / M. Jeremie Yoder)

U.S. Sailors prepare EA-6B Prowler aircraft assigned to the Black Ravens of Electronic Attack Squadron 135 for launch aboard the nuclear-powered aircraft carrier USS *Nimitz* (CVN 68), which was under way in the Pacific Ocean operating in the U.S. 7th Fleet area of responsibility on 12 May 2008. (U.S. Navy / Orrin Batiste)

An EA-6B Prowler assigned to the "Black Ravens" of Electronic Attack Squadron (VAQ) 135 taxis to a catapult aboard the nuclear-powered aircraft carrier USS *Nimitz* (CVN 68) on 11 April 2008. *Nimitz* is operating as part of the U.S. 7th Fleet in the western Pacific and Indian oceans. (U.S. Navy / John Wagner)

An EA-6B Prowler from the "Patriots" of Electronic Attack Squadron (VAQ) 140 launches off the flight deck of USS *Dwight D. Eisenhower* (CVN 69) during flight operations in the Atlantic Ocean on 2 August 2007. (U.S. Navy / Rafael Figueroa Medina)

An EA-6B Prowler assigned to the "Patriots" of Electronic Attack Squadron One Four Zero (VAQ-140), performs a touch and go aboard the Nimitz-class aircraft carrier USS *Dwight D. Eisenhower* (CVN 69) on 29 April 2006. *Eisenhower* and embarked Carrier Air Wing Seven were underway conducting their Composite Training Unit Exercise (COMPTUEX). (U.S. Navy / Dale Miller)

An F-14B Tomcat from Fighter Squadron One Zero Two (VF-102) prepares for launch from USS *George Washington* (CVN 73) in the Arabian Gulf on 4 February 1998. (U.S. Navy / Brian Fleske)

An F-14D Tomcat assigned to the "Tomcatters" of Fighter Squadron Three One (VF-31) makes and arrested landing aboard USS *Theodore Roosevelt* (CVN 71) on 16 January 2006. (U.S. Navy / Sheldon Rowley)

An F-14 "Tomcat" from the "Jolly Rogers" of Fighter Squadron One Zero Three (VF-103) launches from the waist catapult of the USS *George Washington* (CVN 73) on 2 September 2002. *Washington* and her embarked Carrier Air Wing Seventeen were on a regularly-scheduled deployment in support of Operation Enduring Freedom. (U. S. Navy / Corey T. Lewis)

An F-14D Tomcat, assigned to the "Tomcatters" of Fighter Squadron Three One (VF-31), launches off the flight deck of USS *Theodore Roosevelt* (CVN 71) on 24 September 2005. *Roosevelt* and embarked Carrier Air Wing Eight (CVW-8) were underway on a regularly scheduled deployment in support of the Global War on Terrorism. (U.S. Navy / Randall Damm)

An A-6E Intruder aircraft taxis along the flight deck of USS *Dwight D. Eisenhower* on 21 August 1983. (CVN-69). (U.S. Navy)

An F-18A Hornet aircraft is positioned on the flight deck of USS *Abraham Lincoln* (CVN-72) shortly after landing on 3 October 1989. The Hornet, and the two A-7E Corsair II aircraft parked on the side, are from the Patuxent River Flight Test Center aboard the carrier to test the vessel's flight deck capabilities. (U.S. Navy / Tracy Lee Didas)

U.S. Navy (USN) personnel prep an A-6E Intruder on the deck of USS *Dwight D. Eisenhower* (CVN-69) on 15 February 1990. The Intruder was painted in an experimental woodland camouflage scheme. (U.S. Navy)

An EA-6B Prowler assigned to the "Cougars" of Tactical Electronic Warfare Squadron One Three Nine (VAQ-139) prepares for an arrested landing on USS *John C. Stennis* (CVN 74) on 19 October 2004. (U.S. Navy / Mark J. Rebilas)

A U.S. Navy C-2A Greyhound aircraft lands aboard USS *Theodore Roosevelt* (CVN 71), under way in the Gulf of Oman on 16 October 2008. The Greyhound, which transports high-priority cargo, mail, and passengers, is assigned to the Fleet Logistics Support Squadron (VRC-40). (U.S. Navy / Nathan Laird)

A C-2A Greyhound, assigned to the "Providers" of Carrier Logistic Support Squadron (VRC) 30, lands on the USS *Nimitz* (CVN 68) on 15 September 2007. (U.S. Navy / Sarah E. Bitter)

An E-2C Hawkeye, assigned to the "Screwtops" of Carrier Airborne Early Warning Squadron One Two Three (VAW-123), conducts a touch-and-go landing on 31 October 2005. (U.S. Navy / Rob Gaston)

Ripples appear on the body of an E-2C Hawkeye, assigned to the "Seahawks" of Carrier Airborne Early Warning Squadron One Two Six (VAW-126), due to the tremendous amount of torque and pressure exerted on the aircraft while landing on the flight deck of USS *Harry S. Truman* (CVN 75) on 11 January 2005. U.S. Navy / Kristopher Wilson)

An F/A-18C Hornet from the "Salty Dogs" of Air Test and Evaluation Squadron Two Three (VX-23), makes the first "trap" aboard the nuclear powered aircraft carrier USS *Ronald Reagan* (CVN 76) as part of the ship's initial flight deck certification process on 24 July 2003. The *Ronald Reagan* was assigned to North Island Naval Station, San Diego, California. (U.S. Navy / Frankie Bridges)

Two Marine final checkers, assigned to the "Silver Eagles" of Marine Fighter Attack Squadron One One Five (VMFA-115), give the "thumbs up" for an F/A-18A Hornet to launch from the flight deck aboard USS *Harry S. Truman* (CVN 75) on 27 February 2005. Carrier Air Wing Three (CVW-3) was embarked aboard Truman providing close air support and conducting intelligence surveillance and reconnaissance over Iraq. (U.S. Navy / Jay C. Pugh)

The center-deck hatch operator signals to the "Shooter" that the catapult steam pressure is at the proper levels for launching an F/A-18C Hornet assigned to the "Blue Diamonds" of Strike Fighter Squadron One Forty Six (VFA-146) on the flight deck aboard USS *Carl Vinson* (CVN 70) on 24 April 2003. *Carl Vinson* and Carrier Air Wing Nine (CVW-9) were participating in the military training exercise Tandem Thrust '03 in the Mariana Island training area. The exercise focused on crisis action planning and execution of contingency response operations. (U.S. Navy / Inez Lawson)

An F/A-18A Hornet aircraft taxis on the flight deck during flight operations aboard the nuclear-powered aircraft carrier USS *Nimitz* (CVN-68) on 15 June 1992. The Hornet's wing tips and tail fins exhibit the high visibility paint scheme of the Naval Air Weapons Center. (U.S. Navy / Bruce Trombecky)

Commander, Carrier Air Wing One Four (CVW-14), lands an F/A-18E Super Hornet assigned to the "Fighting Redcocks" of Strike Fighter Squadron Two Two (VFA-22) on the flight deck aboard the USS *Ronald Reagan* (CVN 76) on 6 January 2006. *Reagan* Carrier Strike Group deployed in support of the global war on terrorism and maritime security operations. This was the maiden deployment for the Navy's newest nuclear-powered aircraft carrier. (U.S. Navy / Gary Prill)

An F/A-18F Super Hornet assigned to the "Jolly Rogers" of Strike Fighter Squadron One Zero Three (VFA-103) prepares for an arrested landing on USS *Harry S. Truman* (CVN 75) on 28 July 2005. *Truman* was conducting carrier qualifications and sustainment operations off of the East Coast. (U.S. Navy / Kristopher Wilson)

An F/A-18E "Super Hornet" assigned to the "Tophatters" of Strike Fighter Squadron One Four (VFA-14) prepares to launch from one of four steam driven catapults on the flight deck of the USS *Nimitz* (CVN 68) on 17 September 2002. (U.S. Navy / Yesenia Rosas)

Squadron troubleshooters and the ship's catapult crew work together to prepare an F/A-18F "Super Hornet," assigned to the "Black Aces" of Strike Fighter Squadron Four One (VFA-41), for launch from one of four steam-powered catapults on the flight deck of USS *Carl Vinson* (CVN 70) on 4 October 2002. The F/A-18F is a two-seated aircraft with the latest electronic and combat technology installed. The *Carl Vinson* was underway off the west coast of the U.S. conducting training operations in preparation for its upcoming regularly scheduled deployment. (U.S. Navy / Inez Lawson)

An SH-60F Seahawk assigned to the War Hawks of Helicopter Anti-Submarine Squadron Ten (HS-10) flies channel guard for USS *Abraham Lincoln* (CVN 72) as she enters San Diego Harbor on 2 May 2003. The *Abraham Lincoln* Carrier Strike Group flew more than 1,600 sorties and expended 1.6 million pounds of ordnance, including 116 Tomahawks, during its deployment in support of Operation Iraqi Freedom. (U.S. Navy / Andrew J. Betting)

On the evening of 24 April 1980 eight U.S. RH-53D helicopters departed the USS *Nimitz* (CVN 68) in the Arabian Sea as part of a secret mission to rescue U.S. hostages being held by Iranian students in Tehran. The aircraft had been painted in sand camouflage and all U.S. national insignia had been removed. Bad weather and mishaps caused the attempt to fail, and eight U.S. servicemen and one Iranian civilian perished in the abortive operation known as "Eagle Claw." (U.S. Navy)

An SH-3A Sea King helicopter from Helicopter Anti-submarine Squadron 9 (HS-9) assigned to Carrier Air Wing 8 (CVW-8) embarked aboard the nuclear-powered aircraft carrier USS *Nimitz* (CVN-68) is seen from the right on 27 June 1981. (U.S. Navy)

A CH-46 Sea Knight assigned to Helicopter Transport Squadron Eleven (CH-11) lifts cargo during a vertical replenishment (VERTREP) with the aircraft carrier USS *Abraham Lincoln* (CVN 72) on 15 March 2003. (U.S. Navy / Lewis Hunsaker)

"Navy 1," an S-3B Viking from the Blue Wolves of Sea Control Squadron Three Five (VS-35), successfully traps aboard USS *Abraham Lincoln* (CVN 72) on 1 May 2003. The aircraft was carrying President George W. Bush. Mr. Bush was the first sitting President to trap aboard an aircraft carrier at sea. The President visited the ship and met with the crew, congratulating them on a "mission accomplished." He also delivered a live address to the nation from the ship. *Lincoln* was returning from deployment of over nine months in the Arabian Gulf. (U.S. Navy / Gabriel Piper)

Catapult shooters signal to launch an S-3B Viking, assigned to the "Scouts" of Sea Control Squadron Two Four (VS-24), from the flight deck of the Nimitz-class aircraft carrier USS *Theodore Roosevelt* (CVN 71) on 7 December 2005. This was VS-24's last deployment due to the squadron being decommissioned in 2007 with the retirement of the S-3B Viking aircraft. *Roosevelt* and embarked Carrier Air Wing Eight (CVW-8) were underway on a regularly-scheduled deployment conducting maritime security operations. (U.S. Navy / Snyder)

An S-3B Viking assigned to the "Blue Wolves" of Sea Control Squadron Thirty Five (VS-35) folds its wings after making an arrested landing aboard USS *John C. Stennis* (CVN 74) on 17 November 2003. *Stennis* and its embarked Carrier Air Wing Fourteen (CVW-14) were at sea conducting Composite Training Unit Exercise (COMPTUEX) in preparation for an upcoming deployment. (U.S. Navy / Mark J. Rebilas)

An Air Anti-submarine Squadron 29 (VS-29) S-3A Viking aircraft catches the crash barricade and an arresting wire on the flight deck of the nuclear-powered aircraft carrier USS *Abraham Lincoln* (CVN-72) on 10 November 1990. The aircraft was unable to make a normal arrested recovery because of a damaged landing gear. (U.S. Navy / Eric Hayhurst)

The USS *George H. W. Bush* (CVN 77) is seen underway from Naval Station Norfolk conducting acceptance trials and the Board of Inspections and Survey tests of the ship's material conditions and readiness on 7 April 2009. (U.S. Navy / Demetrius L. Patton)

An F/A-18C Hornet of Air Test and Evaluation Squadron (VX) 23 launches from USS *George H. W. Bush* (CVN 77) on 19 May 2009, *Bush's* first day of flight operations. *George H. W. Bush* is the tenth and final Nimitz-class carrier. (U.S. Navy / Dominique J. Moore)

The USS *George H. W. Bush* (CVN 77) is seen during its testing period on 7 April 2009. (U.S. Navy / Demetrius L. Patton)

An Air Test and Evaluation Squadron (VX) 23 F/A-18F Super Hornet makes the first arrested landing on USS *George H. W. Bush* (CVN 77), 19 May 2009. (U.S. Navy / Michael Tackitt)